Wellbeing In My Pocket

Emma Jane

Disclaimer

The ideas and practices shared in this book are intended to inspire and support your personal wellbeing journey. They are not a substitute for professional medical advice, diagnosis, or treatment. Always consult with a qualified healthcare professional before making any changes to your physical or mental health care routine, especially if you are dealing with physical or mental health conditions or taking medication. The author is not responsible for any consequences resulting from the use of the information provided in this book. If you are struggling or feel at risk, seek help from a qualified professional.

Copyright © Emma Jane 2025
All rights reserved. No part of this book may be reproduced or transmitted in any form or by any means, electronic or mechanical, including photocopying, recording, or any information storage or retrieval system, without prior permission in writing from the author. When sharing any part of this work, please credit the author.

Contents

Disclaimer 2

Introduction 6

1. Set Boundaries 14
2. Hydrate 15
3. Food is Medicine 16
4. Morning Routine 18
5. Intention 19
6. Write a "NO" List 20
7. Body Work 22
8. Get Away From It All 24
9. Accept What Is 25
10. Rest 26
11. Self-Acknowledgement 28
12. Learn Something New 29
13. Managing Stress 30
14. Less Is More 32
15. Growth Mindset 34
16. Sunshine 36
17. Feel Your Feelings 38
18. The Only Constant Is Change 39

19. Prioritise Fun 40
20. Gut Health 41
21. Unplug 42
22. Practice Gratitude 44
23. Supplementation 45
24. Self-Compassion 46
25. Connection and Belonging 48
26. Nap 50
27. Use Your Voice 51
28. Move Your Body 52
29. Something to Look Forward To 54
30. Pause 55
31. Soothe Your Senses 56
32. Grounding 58
33. Forgive Yourself 60
34. Flow 61
35. Be Kind 62
36. Reframe 63
37. Eating an Elephant 64
38. Fuel Your Brain 65
39. Inner Child 66

40. Banish the Word Busy 68
41. Reflect 69
42. Be Present 70
43. Replenish 72
44. Do What Lights You Up 73
45. Seek Support 74
46. Explore Somewhere New 75
47. Tune In 76
48. Focus on What You Can Control 78
49. Music 79
50. Sleep Sanctuary 80
51. Treat Yourself 82
52. Prayer Jar 83
Notes 84
Final Thoughts 88
Acknowledgements 90
About The Author 91
References 92

Introduction

Within the pages of this book are the transformative gems gathered from my decade-long journey of health and wellness. During that time, I found myself on a real-world crash course in wellbeing, one I hadn't consciously signed up for, and couldn't seem to opt out of! Through lived experience, I came to understand just how many factors shape human health and how profoundly important wellbeing is.

Perhaps, like me, you struggle at times to maintain a manageable balance between work, life, and family. It can feel like there aren't enough hours in the day, and your needs, wants, and desires come last on a long list of responsibilities. You might find it hard to switch off, constantly rushing, and unable to properly wind down. Perhaps you reach for unhealthy food and drink options for the convenience, comfort, or quick energy boost they provide. At times, it might feel like you're on autopilot, chasing a life we're conditioned to want, without stopping to ask yourself if it truly fulfils you. You could be nearing burnout, but the need for income makes change feel impossible. Maybe you're dealing with health issues, emotional struggles, or feel out of alignment with what matters most to you. You may already be living a life you love and are simply ready to enhance it. Whatever the reason, I'm glad you're here.

The World Health Organisation describes wellbeing as a positive state that includes physical health and reflects quality of life, a sense of purpose, and the ability to cope with challenges. In essence, wellbeing is feeling good, functioning well, and maintaining meaningful connections.

Beyond that, wellbeing is the foundation of how we live. It underpins our habits, choices, and daily practices. It's reflected in how we think, what we say, how we connect with others, and how we respond to conflict and adversity. Wellbeing shapes the way we communicate, the relationships we nurture, and the resilience we build. It encompasses how we care for our bodies through sleep, nutrition, and movement, and how we support ourselves during times of stress and change.

When we understand and prioritise all aspects of our wellbeing, we give ourselves the best chance to function at our fullest capacity. To feel good, build rich relationships, live a soul-nourishing life, and, ultimately, to thrive.

The wellbeing journey is profoundly personal. We each have unique circumstances, genetic constitution, and bio-individuality. As such, wellbeing practices will, and should, look different for each of us. What works beautifully for one person may not be as effective for the next. It's an evolving exploration of self-discovery to find what genuinely nurtures and supports you through the varying seasons of your life.

My wellbeing journey began in 2011 after catastrophic flooding devastated the town where we lived in Queensland, Australia, and I became severely unwell. What started as an upset stomach escalated into food sensitivities, daily abdominal pain, rashes, fevers, heart palpitations, dizziness, brain fog, nausea, thyroid issues, malaise, weight loss, inflammation, severe anxiety, and more. For several years, doctors struggled to find the cause. I was referred to psychiatrists and did my best to carry on, but the symptoms worsened until I could barely function. Finally, in 2015, with the help of my twelfth doctor, I began to get answers and proper treatment.

Over the next four years, supported by several more doctors, I was diagnosed with multiple systemic infections and Chronic Inflammatory Response Syndrome (CIRS). That marked the beginning of an arduous and often overwhelming journey to slowly and painstakingly reclaim my health, which I eventually did, with the help of various therapies, practitioners, and lifestyle changes.

Truthfully, though, I cannot blame the floods alone for my health crisis. My ill health followed years of work and life-related chronic stress, nervous system dysregulation, and burnout. It also coincided with the beginning of a long and deeply challenging infertility journey.

In the early stages of my healing, a trusted mentor, Nicole Cody, encouraged me to think of myself as a champion racehorse. She reminded me that racehorses receive meticulous care and attention. They are fed a specific, high-quality diet to fuel their bodies. They are sponged down after workouts and groomed daily. Their training is carefully balanced to build strength, prevent injury, and support mental focus. They also receive comprehensive health support. When cared for in this way, racehorses perform exceptionally well. Nicole proposed that I would too, given the same kind of special care and treatment. She gently suggested that if I took excellent care of myself physically, mentally, emotionally and spiritually, I'd perform well in every area of my life.

I had never considered that I might need to care for myself with such dedication. My health crisis forced me to face some uncomfortable truths. I couldn't keep ignoring my body, pushing past its limits, or repeating the same patterns. It was a turning point. I began to pay attention to the subtle cues I'd long overridden. I slowly learnt to honour what my body was trying to tell me, and I began to understand what needed to change.

Through this process, I've come to see that health and wellbeing are far more layered than I'd once thought. They are not only about eating well, exercising, and indulging in the occasional treat, although that is certainly part of it. True wellbeing is constantly evolving and lies in the habits and behaviours that we quietly embed into our everyday life.

The strategies I share here are the ones I have gradually discovered that work well for me. Much of this was through trial and error. Others were inspired by books, blogs, podcasts, and the many people who helped me along the way. A reference list is included at the end of the book. I hope that some of these practices will resonate with you or that they will inspire you to explore the habits and ways of being that will be uniquely supportive and effective for you.

You might choose to follow the weekly strategies in order, or you may prefer to read through the book and focus only on those that resonate most with you. Another approach is to use the book intuitively. Hold it in your hands and ask, "What aspect of wellbeing would be beneficial for me to consider this week?" Then open to a random page. If a particular strategy keeps coming up, trust that it's what you need and keep working with it. At the back of the book, you'll find a few pages for your notes and reflections.

I wish you every success on your wellbeing journey. Go gently with yourself. We live this life once, in this body, with this story, and it is over before we know it. Others may walk beside us at times, but you are the only one who travels your path from beginning to end. It is worth knowing yourself well, being your own best friend, greatest advocate, and most devoted carer. You are so precious, and more loved than you know.

" It is health that is real wealth and not pieces of gold and silver."

- Mahatma Gandhi

The Weekly Strategies

1. Set Boundaries

Time and energy are two of our most valuable resources, yet we often overlook them or freely give them away. Daily life is filled with the constant pull of demands, and when we consistently give away to others what we need for ourselves, it can leave us feeling depleted, time-poor, and even resentful.

Boundaries help us decide what is okay for us and what is not. We can set boundaries around various aspects of our lives, including our time, work, relationships, emotions, and physical and mental capacities. Being discerning and protective of where we invest our time and energy is not only okay, it's essential. Saying no to others and yes to ourselves is a powerful way to affirm that our needs matter.

ACTION STEP: Take a mindful approach to your commitments and interactions. Tune into the week ahead. What's on your schedule? How are your energy levels? Give yourself permission to prioritise what feels good for you. Spend less time engaging with people or activities that deplete your energy and more time engaging with what uplifts and replenishes you.

Setting boundaries, saying no, and making yourself unavailable when your time and energy are limited is okay. Protecting your energy isn't selfish. It's a way to ensure you're at your best for yourself and those who matter most.

2. Hydrate

Water is vital for life, yet many of us don't drink enough of it. While it quenches thirst, adequate hydration also plays a crucial role in supporting brain function and overall health. It aids digestion, helps regulate body temperature, assists in detoxification, and ensures the smooth operation of nearly every cellular process. Even mild dehydration can lead to fatigue, headaches, and difficulty concentrating.

ACTION STEP: The formula below provides a baseline for your ideal daily water intake. Needs may vary depending on activity levels, climate, and overall health, so listen to your body and adjust accordingly.

- **In kilograms**: multiply your weight by 0.033.

- **In pounds**: multiply your weight by 0.67

To optimise hydration, consider adding a good-quality electrolyte to your water. Electrolytes like sodium, potassium, and magnesium enhance the electrical charge across cell membranes, helping fluids absorb more effectively into cells. Without them, what you drink may pass through your system too quickly to provide full hydration benefits.

Coconut water is a natural source of electrolytes and can serve as a good alternative, or simply add a small pinch of natural sea salt to your glass.

3. Food Is Medicine

"Let food be thy medicine and medicine be thy food" is a quote attributed to Hippocrates, an ancient Greek physician who shifted medicine away from superstitious beliefs toward a more scientific approach. He focused on understanding the natural causes of illness and the importance of a balanced diet, regular exercise, and fresh air in maintaining good health. The Hippocratic Oath is still used today and emphasises patient wellbeing, confidentiality and avoiding harm.

Many of us are fortunate to have a wide variety of delicious foods readily available, but not everything that tastes good is good for us. Choosing simple, nutrient-dense foods such as fresh fruits, vegetables, high-quality protein, and healthy fats is a powerful way to enhance our health. These foods provide essential vitamins, minerals, and antioxidants that nourish the body, support the immune system, and promote overall wellbeing.

It's important because:

- Foods high in sugar and refined carbohydrates can cause blood sugar spikes followed by crashes, leaving you feeling tired and moody.

- Additives and preservatives in processed foods can disrupt gut health, which plays a key role in digestion, immunity, and mental health.

- Nutrient-dense foods help maintain steady energy levels and support brain function.

- Many chronic health conditions are closely linked to diet.
- Certain foods contain bioactive compounds with anti-inflammatory, antioxidant, and healing properties.

ACTION STEP: Eat healthy, whole, unprocessed foods, such as fruits, vegetables, high-quality proteins, and healthy fats. Use herbs and spices like garlic, ginger, and turmeric for their medicinal properties. Avoid consuming processed foods high in sugar, salt, additives, and unhealthy fats.

Notice how you feel after eating. Are you energised and focused, or do you feel bloated, sluggish and tired? Pay attention when you reach for food. Are you eating because your body needs fuel, or is it due to boredom, stress, or a difficult emotion? Try a "swap and savour" approach, replace one processed food item with a whole food each day. For example, swap chips for a handful of nuts, or soft drink for sparkling water with a squeeze of lemon or lime. Seek the help of a qualified dietitian if you need support.

4. Morning Routine

The way we start the morning can significantly influence the rest of our day. Some days, we wake up feeling energised, optimistic, and ready to tackle whatever lies ahead. At other times, we may feel groggy and unmotivated, struggling to shake off that lingering fatigue. Establishing a consistent morning routine can help transform any start into something more positive, regardless of how we initially feel.

My morning routine often begins with a glass of warm water and a squeeze of lemon. This simple ritual helps to rehydrate the body, kick-start digestion, support detoxification, and balance pH levels after sleep. After that, I head out for a walk with my dog to enjoy the morning sunlight, breathe the fresh air, and connect with nature. During this time, I practice gratitude and set intentions for the day ahead. This routine helps to create a smooth transition from sleep to wakefulness and eases me into the day.

ACTION STEP: Take a moment to evaluate your morning routine. How does it prepare you for the day ahead? Are there any aspects you could modify? Start with one small change and let it evolve organically over time, creating a morning routine that works for you.

5. Intention

When we set a clear intention, we direct our thoughts and energy toward a desired experience, emotional state, or outcome. Our mindset and beliefs shape how we move through and experience the world. By approaching each day with conscious awareness, we increase our ability to create the kind of experiences we want and enable the universe to support us.

This practice can be simple. You might take a moment during your morning commute to set an intention for the day, saying something like, "I intend to make a positive difference today." It could also be more specific, such as, "I intend to complete my project today."

At its core, setting an intention is about deciding how you want to feel, respond, and focus your energy.

ACTION STEP: This week, reflect on the intentions behind your actions and interactions. Why do you do what you do? What are you endeavouring to experience or create? Set intentions for your day, your week, your interactions and relationships. Intention can be the difference between going through the motions and taking inspired action toward the life that you want.

6. Write a "NO" List

If you find yourself saying "yes" to things you'd rather decline, fulfilling commitments out of obligation or honouring agreements that your 'past self' made, even though they no longer feel right for you. If you're feeling overstretched, low on energy, or time-poor, it might be worth creating a "NO" list.

A very wise colleague shared this principle with me, and it can be found in the book *Forty Favours the Brave* by Lisa Carlaw and Sarah Wills. It serves as a personal blueprint, where you identify activities, habits, or commitments that drain your energy, no longer serve you, or simply don't bring you joy. You don't need to justify your choices to anyone. Life is too short to be spent feeling resentful or overburdened.

Everyone's "NO" list will look different, but examples might include:

- No answering calls if you prefer texting
- No screen time after 8 p.m.
- No work emails outside office hours
- No weeknight commitments
- No phone in the bedroom
- No alcohol on weekdays

ACTION STEP: Give yourself permission to honestly assess what isn't working for you. Start by choosing a few non-negotiables to include on your "NO" list. Remember that this list is a living document. Refine it as you go and watch how it makes a difference! You could use the space below to begin exploring the habits or routines that are no longer serving you.

7. Body Work

Our bodies hold onto more than we realise, including past experiences, emotions, and thoughts. Chronic stress, unresolved trauma, and everyday challenges can manifest in the body in a myriad of ways, including muscle tightness, joint pain, digestive issues, illness, and fatigue.

Bodywork therapies such as chiropractic care, massage, and acupuncture offer practical ways to release stored tension, improve circulation, and restore balance to your nervous system. Somatic exercises (like stretching and movement) and breath work (like diaphragmatic breathing) can help release the emotional tension held in the body and calm the stress response.

ACTION STEP: Reflect on what helps your body to let go of stress and feel at ease. If you have a favourite practice, schedule time to prioritise it at home or by making regular appointments with a practitioner or attending a class. If you're feeling adventurous, explore a new modality and see how your body responds. Tune into your body's signals and find different ways that enable it to relax and let go.

Consider:

- Yoga, Pilates or Tai Chi: Which combine mindful movement and breathwork to release tension, increase flexibility, and calm the mind.

- Lying with your legs up the wall: Can relieve stress and balance the nervous system.

- Foam Rolling or Self-Massage: Can relieve muscle soreness and improve circulation.

- Meditation: Can help to calm the mind and relax the body.

- Epsom Salt Baths: The magnesium in Epsom salts can relax muscles, aid in detoxification, and soothe the nervous system.

- Moving to music: Can help release stored stress and tension.

8. Get Away from It All

It can be challenging to fully relax in your own environment where there are chores to do, errands to run, and many other distractions. Getting away from it all by physically removing yourself from your usual surroundings is a chance to switch off and simply "be" without the weight of your everyday routines and responsibilities.

When you change your environment and create space away, you allow for new experiences, fresh energy, ideas, and perspectives, as well as moments of freedom and inspiration to find you.

ACTION STEP: Plan intentional time away to immerse yourself in a different environment. This could be a day trip, a short getaway, or a holiday. Whether it's a tiny house in the forest, a beautiful beach, or a bustling city you've always wanted to visit, be sure to disconnect. Let others know you're away and won't be available, and focus on yourself. Let this be your time to relax and enjoy.

9. Accept What Is

Sometimes, what's happening in our lives is incredibly difficult to accept, but resisting reality can create even more suffering, tension, and stress. It's only natural to push back against discomfort, to feel upset by injustice, and to resist change. Often, we are justified in taking action, seeking to correct misunderstandings, and standing up for what's right.

However, if you've exhausted every avenue and your mental health is paying the price, it may be time to consider the power of acceptance. For the sake of your peace of mind, let go of the struggle against what is, and shift your focus inward. Seek support from a trusted professional, engage in regular self-care, and invite calm into your life through practices like prayer, meditation, or quiet reflection.

When we constantly fight life, life usually wins. Sometimes, the most healing thing we can do is to drop the rope and choose a path of lesser resistance.

ACTION STEP: Identify a situation where you've been resistant and feeling stuck or powerless. Take a moment to ponder the steps you've taken to bring about shift, healing, or change. Then, set an intention to release the weight of this burden, whether by speaking it aloud, writing it down and burning it safely, or offering it up in prayer. Reflect on how you can best care for and support yourself, your own heart, and your mental health as you move forward.

10. Rest

We can think we are rested depending on the quality of our sleep, but sleep and rest are not the same thing. Saundra Dalton-Smith describes seven key forms of rest in her book *Sacred Rest*, each playing an essential role in how we recharge.

1. Physical Rest: Of which there are two types: **passive rest,** which includes sleep & napping, and **active rest,** which includes yoga, stretching, and massage.

2. Mental Rest: Prevents cognitive overload by incorporating short, intentional breaks throughout the day. This can include stepping away from the task at hand, going outside, and focusing on your surroundings.

3. Sensory Rest: Means taking a break from constant stimulation, such as screens, noise, and bright lights. It involves intentionally unplugging and creating quiet, calm spaces to give your senses a chance to recover.

4. Creative Rest: Encompasses the arts and creative pursuits, such as baking, sewing, gardening, and woodwork.

5. Emotional Rest: Intentionally taking a break from the emotional demands of life includes disconnecting from things that cause stress, expressing emotions in healthy ways, stepping away from emotionally draining people and situations, and focusing on small things that

bring contentment, relaxation and rejuvenation.

6. Social Rest: Disconnecting from the world and taking time for yourself. It also includes spending time with people who feel good to be around and help recharge your energy.

7. Spiritual Rest: This is the ability to connect beyond the physical and mental, and feel a deep sense of belonging, love, acceptance and purpose. To experience this, engage in something greater than yourself. Explore spirituality through books and teachers, or by joining a church or community group. Spend quiet time journaling and reflecting, or simply spend time in the great outdoors.

ACTION STEP: Take time to consider which types of rest you currently engage in, and where you might add some additional rest from the list above.

11. Self-Acknowledgement

The simple act of regularly acknowledging yourself is a powerful tool for building a more positive self-perception and supporting your mental health. Each time you recognise an achievement, notice something you've done well, or positively reflect on how you navigated your day and interactions with others, you strengthen your sense of self-worth, self-belief, and confidence.

This isn't about big-noting yourself; it's a gentle, consistent practice that activates the brain's reward system, releasing feel-good chemicals like serotonin and dopamine that naturally lift your mood and support a more positive mindset.

Over time, as you intentionally look for your strengths and successes, you're training your brain to see the good in yourself. As you continue to acknowledge yourself, your sense of self-worth will quietly grow, shaping how you meet challenges, relate to others and carry yourself each day.

ACTION STEP: Before bed each night, think of something you can acknowledge yourself for. What went well today? What are you proud of? What progress did you make? Write it down or say it silently to yourself. Choose a regular time to reflect on your week. Consider journaling about moments that made you feel proud or fulfilled. By taking time to recognise your progress and efforts, you're boosting your mental health and cultivating a more positive, empowered mindset.

12. Learn Something New

Learning brings meaning and richness to life. It sparks curiosity, inspires new ideas, and helps us adapt and grow. Each time we learn something new, the brain forms fresh connections, strengthening neural pathways and supporting long-term brain health. Exploring things that interest us can lead to insights we didn't expect, thoughtful ideas, valuable connections, and a deeper understanding of the world.

ACTION STEP: What are you curious about or interested in? It could be anything from learning a language to taking an art class or playing an instrument. Perhaps there is a short course or a book on a subject you've wanted to explore? Choose something new to learn about and immerse yourself in the experience.

13. Managing Stress

Stress is the body's natural response to too much mental or emotional pressure. While some stress is normal, chronic or unmanaged stress can take a significant physical and psychological toll. Over time, elevated cortisol and adrenaline can disrupt the nervous system. This affects mood, energy, sleep, digestion, hormones, and relationships, leading to exhaustion and burnout. The key to managing stress isn't about eliminating it entirely but building awareness and responding to it effectively. If you are noticing signs of stress, know that it's your body's way of asking for support. You may observe:

- moodiness or irritability
- angry outbursts
- excessive worry or ruminating thoughts
- feeling overwhelmed
- headaches
- tearfulness
- sweating
- changes in appetite (over- or under-eating)
- not sleeping well
- muscle tension
- increased heart rate
- difficulty coping with usual everyday tasks

In times of peak stress, it's easy for healthy habits and routines to fall away. But a little foresight and flexibility can help you find balance. This might look like preparing easy meals, letting go of non-essential tasks and commitments, asking for support, or thinking differently to relieve pressure. Prioritise self-care in whatever way supports you, whether that's more sleep, gentle movement, time in nature, or time alone. You don't need to push through, and you don't need to do it all by yourself.

ACTION STEP: Take a moment to reflect on how stress is showing up for you. What would help you feel more supported? Perhaps it would be beneficial to under-commit, delegate tasks more effectively, or reconsider your expectations of yourself and others. Consider taking a day off if you need one, or using an app such as Headspace, Liven, or Smiling Mind to support you through.

14. Less Is More

It's easy to fall into the trap of thinking that doing more work, having more commitments, and adding more to the to-do list means we will get more done. Unfortunately, this 'more is more' approach often leads to stress, overwhelm, and a feeling of constantly rushing, rather than feelings of calm and being in control.

We begin to reclaim space to breathe when we embrace the principle that less is more. By intentionally taking on fewer tasks or social engagements than we might be capable of handling, we ensure that what is on our plate is manageable, balanced, and sustainable.

ACTION STEP: Take a moment to evaluate: Where are you taking on too much? Where can you create more space? Where can you let go of unnecessary obligations and stop spreading yourself so thin?

Consider some of the following:

- Outsource or delegate: Hire household help, use meal kits or delivery services.

- Embrace convenience: Buy pre-chopped veggies and batch-cook meals.

- Let go of perfectionism: not everything needs to be perfect to be good enough.

- Reclaim time for yourself: Block out time on your calendar for yourself, even just to do nothing!

Simplifying is not about doing less for the sake of it. It's about creating room for ease over exhaustion and prioritising your peace and your energy. Less isn't actually about less. It's about more! More freedom, more flexibility, and more fulfilment.

15. Growth Mindset

Those with a growth mindset tend to view challenges as opportunities and setbacks as valuable learning experiences. They understand that trial and error are essential for mastery and that progress comes from learning over time.

A growth mindset fosters resilience, helps us be more adaptable, increases our chance of success, and can reduce stress and anxiety by helping us deal with disappointment and frustration in healthier ways.

ACTION STEP:

- Cultivate curiosity: Be open to learning new things. Ask questions, explore new subjects, and meet new people.

- Reframe 'failure' as learning: Instead of beating yourself up, focus on what you learnt and how you will move forward.

- Seek feedback: From colleagues, friends, and loved ones so you can reflect and improve.

- Pay attention to what you're consuming: Instead of scrolling on your device or watching trashy TV, listen to an uplifting podcast or read something inspiring or educational.

- Stay persistent: Be patient. Remember that change and growth take time.

- Adjust and adapt: Be willing to adjust your sails along the way.

- Celebrate small wins: Growth is a continuous process, and it's important to celebrate along the way.

16. Sunshine

A little time in the sun can do wonders for how we feel. While it's well-known that Vitamin D plays a crucial role in our health, sunlight also triggers the production of beta-endorphins in the skin. These natural chemicals help reduce pain, regulate stress, and increase happiness, providing a biological boost that extends beyond the warmth we feel on our skin. Some additional benefits of soaking up the sun include:

- Boosts mood and promotes a sense of wellbeing: Sunlight can help brighten your outlook by increasing feel-good hormones.

- Strengthens the immune system: Exposure to sunlight supports your body's natural defences.

- Promotes relaxation: Reduces cortisol levels and promotes a sense of calm.

- Aids in healing: Sunlight supports the body's natural ability to repair itself.

- Enhances alertness: Sunlight can help you feel more energised and awake.

- Reduces depression: Regular sunlight exposure may alleviate symptoms of mild depression.

- Improves sleep: Sunlight helps regulate serotonin and melatonin, two hormones critical for restful sleep.

In his book *Sleep Smarter*, Shawn Stevenson explains that our eyes have light receptors that signal to the body that it's time to wake up and tell the brain to kick-start the production of serotonin, the feel-good hormone. Serotonin also plays a key role in regulating our sleep cycle. It's a precursor to melatonin, the hormone that helps us wind down and sleep more soundly at night. By getting sunlight in the morning, you're not just boosting your mood for the day ahead; you're also setting yourself up for better sleep at night.

ACTION STEP: Catch at least 10 minutes of morning sunshine without your sunglasses on! You don't have to go far. Step outside for a quick walk, sip your morning coffee on the patio, or stand and breathe in the light at a window. Let those first rays of sunlight support your body's natural rhythm. Take advantage of sunny moments throughout the day, even if it's just for a few minutes. A little sunshine can go a long way in boosting your mood, your energy, and your sleep! Remember to be sun-safe when spending extended time outdoors.

17. Feel Your Feelings

Feelings can be overwhelming, often surfacing at inconvenient moments. It's natural to want to control, suppress, or ignore them, but unprocessed emotions can manifest as stress, physical pain, or illness.

Taking the time to process your feelings doesn't have to be complicated. Simple practices such as walking, journaling, or sitting quietly and observing your emotions can make a significant difference.

Begin by naming the emotion and noticing where in your body you feel it. Next, notice the sensations, see if you can name or describe them. Allow them to exist without judging them, and without trying to figure them out or assigning a story to them. This gentle acknowledgment can begin the process of release and healing.

ACTION STEP: Create space in your life to gently feel your feelings. When emotions arise, sit with them. Place a hand on your body where you notice the feeling. Use a few words to describe the sensation. For example, an anxious feeling in the tummy, when examined more closely, may feel like champagne bubbles. Breathe deeply. Allow the sensations to dissipate as you explore and describe them. Offer yourself kindness as you move through the experience. Work with an experienced practitioner for further support.

18. The Only Constant Is Change

Change is an inevitable part of life. While it can be daunting, it also offers opportunities for growth, fresh energy, and exciting new beginnings. It's a chance for a reset, a reminder that things can, and do, improve and evolve. However, adjusting to change isn't always easy. It might feel uncomfortable at first or unfold in unexpected ways, bringing uncertainty and challenges.

ACTION STEP: As you navigate change, give yourself time and space to adjust. If things don't unfold as expected, try gently shifting your perspective. Focus on what you've gained rather than what you've lost, and consider how things might be different or even better than before. Sometimes change begins with how you choose to think, and if things still don't feel right, take practical steps towards making a different choice.

19. Prioritise Fun

Having fun isn't just for kids; it's a key ingredient for living a healthy, balanced life. Fun helps us unwind, boosts mood, and lowers stress by calming the nervous system and increasing feel-good hormones. Fun can strengthen our relationships with others and create space for deeper connections. Taking time to laugh, play and have fun brings lightness to the moment and makes our soul sing!

ACTION STEP: Who and what do you find fun? Reflect on what truly makes you laugh and come alive. Commit to scheduling moments of fun into your week. Whether it's connecting with someone you love, trying a new activity, or revisiting a favourite thing to do. Balance your responsibilities with intentional moments of laughter and play. Life feels lighter when we make room for fun!

20. Gut Health

Our gut breaks down the food we eat, absorbs nutrients to support the body, and houses 70% of the immune system! Many aspects of modern life can impact the gut microbiome, including high or chronic stress levels, insufficient sleep, consumption of processed foods and drinks, and the use of certain medications.

When the gut is not in peak condition, our ability to absorb nutrients from food is reduced. This disruption also weakens immune function and interferes with hormone regulation. Additionally, it may lead to decreased production of neurotransmitters, which can negatively affect mental health.

Improving your diet and repairing your gut microbiome may alleviate brain fog, low energy, mood issues, and numerous other health and digestive problems.

ACTION STEP: Think 80/20; it's what we do most of the time that counts. Reduce processed foods and drinks such as chips, biscuits, sweets, soft drinks, and alcohol, as these can be gut-damaging and inflammatory. Eat healthier, whole foods, such as berries, vegetables, nuts, good fats like avocado and olive oil, and protein. Organic broth and high-quality probiotics can also be effective in healing and soothing the gut. Work with a qualified practitioner to tailor your own individualised gut healing plan.

21. Unplug

In today's world, we are rarely ever truly "off." Devices keep us constantly connected to work, other people, and to what's happening on a global scale, making it hard to relax properly. There was a time when leaving the office meant we were unreachable until the next workday, or being away from home meant we could fully disconnect from all contact and obligations.

Responsiveness to alerts and being constantly "switched on" and available overstimulates the nervous system, keeping us in a heightened state. In his book *The Connected Species*, Mark Williams outlines how notifications trigger the brain's reward system, giving us a tiny hit of dopamine even if the alert is meaningless. He notes that the unpredictability of notifications, not knowing when they'll arrive or whether they'll be important, creates anticipation and keeps us checking. This taps into our fight-or-flight response. Tech developers use this knowledge to engineer their apps and devices to be addictive.

Humans need downtime away from stimulation and information to allow the nervous system to regulate.

ACTION STEP: Set clear boundaries with your phone and other devices. Consider limiting your availability to certain hours, such as 8 a.m. to 8 p.m. Designate one day a week as a device-free day. Set app timers, switch off non-essential notifications, and hide apps from your home screen. Alternatively, if you're feeling courageous, you could uninstall some apps from your phone altogether. Experiment with what works best for you, prioritise unplugged time to reset your nervous system and recharge your body and mind. Consider what you will do instead of being on your device. Will you read a book, connect with a loved one, do something creative, or spend time with your pets? The options are endless!

22. Practice Gratitude

Practising gratitude means noticing the positives, the blessings, what you do have, what is working well, and all you have to be thankful for. This doesn't mean pretending that life is easy, or ignoring the challenges you face; it's about noticing the beauty that exists alongside them. It means focusing on what's going well, the kindness you've received, and the abundance you already have. It's a way of shifting perspective, even on the hard days, to recognise that amidst the struggles, there are things to be thankful for.

Regularly practising gratitude can play a key role in rewiring neural pathways, thus creating a more positive outlook as your default. Over time, this subtle but powerful shift impacts your mindset and overall wellbeing. Your emotional resilience, physical health, and mental clarity all benefit from this simple practice.

The beauty of gratitude is that even the smallest moments, like a warm hug or the cosiness of your bed, can fill your heart when you take the time to notice them.

ACTION STEP: At the end of each day, reflect. Think of five things that you're grateful for and why. They might be big, like an opportunity that came your way, or small, like a smile from a stranger. Maybe it's the taste of your meal, the way your pet greets you, or the sound of someone's laugh. Allow yourself to feel the warmth of those moments as you drift off to sleep.

23. Supplementation

The body is a unique and beautifully complex system with needs that differ from person to person. If you're experiencing low energy, mood fluctuations, challenges in managing stress, or just not feeling yourself, these may be signals of underlying biochemical imbalances. Factors like nutrient deficiencies, hormonal fluctuations, or inflammation can all play a role in how you feel, but the good news is that they're often identifiable and easily addressed.

Regular blood work with a trusted doctor is one of the most effective ways to uncover potential imbalances in your body. Tests for essential nutrients such as vitamin D, B12, magnesium, and iron, as well as markers for thyroid function, adrenal function, hormone levels, and inflammation, can provide valuable insights into your health.

Beyond traditional healthcare, Naturopaths focus on understanding the body holistically and can offer personalised guidance on supplementation, diet, and lifestyle strategies tailored to your unique needs to restore balance and improve energy levels.

ACTION STEP: Take the first step toward feeling your best by scheduling an appointment with a healthcare practitioner to review your blood work. Partner with your doctor, and if appropriate, a qualified naturopath, to explore personalised support and supplementation that can bring your body back to balance.

24. Self-Compassion

Self-compassion is the ability to offer yourself the same understanding, kindness, and non-judgment that you'd naturally extend to a friend who is struggling or feeling down. It means turning inward with care and support when you're facing challenges rather than being harsh or self-critical.

Doctor Kristin Neff, a pioneer in self-compassion research, highlights that self-compassion is not self-pity or indulgence. Instead, it's a balanced approach to caring for yourself that fosters emotional resilience and improved mental health. She notes that as mammals, we are wired to respond to warmth, gentle touch, and soft, soothing vocalisations. Her research identifies three core elements of self-compassion:

1. Self-Kindness: Being warm and understanding toward yourself. Offering soothing words and actions rather than being critical.

2. Common Humanity: Acknowledging that we all experience suffering, failure and imperfection at times and are not alone in our struggles.

3. Mindfulness: Observing emotions with curiosity and openness, rather than suppressing them or exaggerating their significance.

ACTION STEP: Practise self-compassion by applying these principles in your daily life. Acknowledge how you're feeling without judgement.

Take a moment to ask yourself, "What would I say to a friend if they were experiencing this?" "How would I comfort or encourage them?" Self-compassion is a skill that deepens with practice. The more you nurture yourself with kindness and understanding, the easier it will become.

25. Connection and Belonging

Basic human needs extend beyond food, water, and shelter. A sense of belonging is equally vital to our wellbeing. The human brain is hard-wired for connection with others. Feeling connected to people, groups, places, and activities that make us feel seen, heard, valued, and appreciated enhances both our mental and emotional health.

Meaningful connections foster emotional security and a sense of purpose. Social ties can serve as a buffer against stress and contribute to overall happiness. Positive connections with others are associated with lower blood pressure, reduced risk of chronic illness, and longer life expectancy. When we feel that we belong and know we have people who love and support us, we become more resilient and better able to navigate whatever life brings our way.

It's the quality of our relationships, not just the quantity that truly impacts our wellbeing. Prioritise time with people who uplift you, who allow space for authenticity, and with whom you feel safe, energised, and respected. Healthy relationships involve give and take. They thrive on authentic communication, mutual care, common interests, and shared experiences. It's okay to step back or set boundaries when relationships start to feel one-sided, draining, or misaligned.

ACTION STEP: Take time to reflect on where and with whom you feel a sense of belonging. Are there certain people, groups, or activities that uplift and energise you? Take a moment to appreciate these sources of connection. Make it a point to connect regularly. Plan a coffee date, a walk in the park, or do something fun together. Consider if your life could benefit from cultivating additional spaces of belonging. For example:

- Join a community: seek out a club, group, or class that aligns with your interests or values.
- Strengthen existing relationships: reach out to a friend or family member you enjoy spending time with.
- Create your own space: host a gathering, organise a book club, or invite someone new for a catch-up.

By reaching out and fostering connections, you not only enhance your own wellbeing but also create a sense of belonging for others.

26. Nap

I have already mentioned rest, however, napping deserves its own spotlight. For years, I powered through no matter how I felt. I've come to realise that honouring the need for a nap when we're tired makes a huge difference to how we feel, function and show up in the world.

Napping can improve energy, mood, and mental clarity by giving the body time to rest, regulate and repair. The Spanish tradition of the afternoon siesta has been valued for generations. Perhaps they've been onto something all along?

ACTION STEP: If you're tired, give yourself permission to stop what you're doing and rest. Suppose you feel like a nap in the middle of the day, after work, in between commitments, or before tackling your to-do list. Honour that need. Be honest with others when you need to take a breather and reschedule plans if necessary. Prioritise downtime and take naps as you need to.

27. Use Your Voice

As social beings, our relationships and how we are perceived are central to our experience. It can be challenging to express our true thoughts and feelings without the fear of damaging those relationships or offending others. Many of us avoid confrontation, and, in doing so, sacrifice our authenticity to maintain peace. However, this can be detrimental in the long run, leading to a disconnect between our true selves and the relationships and perceptions others have of us that we are trying to preserve.

By not expressing ourselves, we may inadvertently perpetuate relationships and situations that are misaligned with our needs and values. Over time, this can cause those relationships to falter. We may also set ourselves up for commitments and duties that are beyond our capacity.

Though it may feel challenging or uncomfortable at first, embracing honesty and authenticity gets easier with practice. The potential benefits, such as greater alignment and more authentic interactions, far outweigh the discomfort in the long run.

ACTION STEP: Take a small step to express your authentic feelings. Whether it's sharing an opinion, setting a limit, or being open about how you feel. Before speaking, consider your intention: What outcome are you hoping for? How would you like each party to feel afterwards? Speak from the heart, stay curious, and ask questions to better understand their perspective. If needed, seek professional guidance or support from a trusted third party.

28. Move Your Body

Movement is a powerful way to support physical, mental, and emotional health. It can also help the body to release built-up stress. Whether it's a gym workout, a restorative yoga session, swimming, cycling, dancing, or taking a walk, many forms of movement will contribute to a healthier, happier you.

Some key reasons to make movement a priority include:

- Boosts mood: Exercise stimulates the release of endorphins, your body's natural feel-good chemicals.

- Supports mental clarity: Physical activity increases blood flow to the brain, which can enhance memory, focus, and overall cognitive function.

- Improves sleep: Engaging in physical activity helps regulate your sleep-wake cycle.

- Strengthens your heart: Regular aerobic activities improve cardiovascular health.

- Fights stress and anxiety: Movement helps reduce cortisol, the primary stress hormone, while increasing serotonin and dopamine levels, the feel-good hormones.

Movement isn't about perfection or intensity; it's about consistency and enjoyment. Discover what feels good for you, and let it become a regular part of your routine. Allow movement to be a celebration of what your body is capable of and what it can do, not a punishment for what it can't.

ACTION STEP: Commit to moving your body in a way that feels enjoyable and accessible for you. Pick something you love or try something new just for fun! If you love music, turn up the volume and dance. If you enjoy nature, take a walk or hike in a local park or along a beach to soak in the calming benefits of being outdoors. If you've been thinking about a fitness class or activity, take the plunge and give it a try!

29. Something to Look Forward To

This was first shared with me by a practitioner when I was very sick, and was brought to mind again recently when a lovely colleague heard it discussed on a *Life Matters* podcast episode. As children, we naturally look forward to simple things like going to a theme park, or a movie and dessert night, but as adults, we can lose this habit amidst our daily responsibilities.

Looking forward to something can instantly uplift your mood, and it has a tangible physiological effect. Anticipation creates positive suspense, releasing dopamine, a feel-good hormone. Research shows we gain more joy from anticipating positive experiences than from material possessions. The good news is that it doesn't have to be extravagant. Finding joy in small, everyday things can make a big difference.

ACTION STEP: Make it a habit to always have something to look forward to. Before bed, ask yourself, "What am I looking forward to tomorrow?" It could be as simple as trying a new recipe, catching up with a friend, getting to bed early, or watching a good TV show. Take it further by planning a meaningful activity for each week, each month, and each year.

30. Pause

Mental health matters just as much as physical health, and sometimes, the most powerful act of self-care is simply "opting out" for a moment. When you find yourself rushing to respond to something you're not sure about, or feeling emotionally overloaded, that's your cue to pause.

Instead of automatically saying yes, pushing through, or meeting others' needs at your own expense, take a moment to check in with yourself. How's your energy? Do you have the time and capacity for what's being asked of you? Is this something you genuinely want to do or just something you feel obligated to say yes to?

Taking time before responding helps you to reconnect with yourself first and then respond to life more intentionally. You don't have to explain or justify yourself. You are allowed to take a moment to slow down and honour your own needs first.

ACTION STEP: When you feel unsure or pulled in too many directions, pause. Take a breath and ask yourself: Do I have the capacity for this? Is this what I truly want? If the answer is no or unclear, permit yourself to say no, or delay responding until you've had time to properly consider things. Check your calendar. If upcoming plans feel draining instead of nourishing, consider rescheduling or releasing them. Let your choices reflect care not just for others, but for yourself, too.

31. Soothe Your Senses

Engaging your senses is a powerful way to bring centeredness to your day. By intentionally focusing on sensory experiences, you can create moments of mindfulness and relaxation that help you feel more present and grounded. I often come home after work and light a candle. This simple ritual signals that it's time to leave the workday behind and settle into the comfort of home.

ACTION STEP: Try incorporating some simple practices, such as:

- Listen to music: Choose a playlist that uplifts your mood or helps you unwind. Let it transport you to a place of calm and happiness.

- Browse through old photos: Looking through cherished memories can evoke positive emotions and help you reconnect with happy times.

- Sip on a delicious beverage: Savour the flavours as you enjoy.

- Use your favourite scent or lotion: Take a moment to apply a fragrance or lotion that you love. Breathe deeply and let the scent envelop you.

- Gaze at a calming scene: Look out the window, at a painting, or the night sky. Allow your eyes to take in the details.

- Taste a piece of chocolate: Slowly savour the richness and complexity of the flavour. Let the chocolate melt in your mouth.

- Practice deep breathing with essential oils: Place a few drops of essential oil on the palms of your hands. Cup your hands over your nose and inhale deeply.

- Diffuse essential oils: Allow the aroma to soothe you.

- Light a candle: To create a sense of peace and ambience.

- Engage your hands: Build something, plant something, bake something, make something, colour something, create something.

- Enjoy a soothing bath: Use Epsom salts and magnesium to relieve tired muscles. Add a few drops of essential oil to create a calming aroma. Light a candle. Let your mind settle.

32. Grounding

As our daily lives have become more fast-paced, we've become increasingly disconnected from nature. Spending so much time indoors, glued to screens, and wearing shoes all the time creates a barrier between us and the natural rhythms of the Earth. This disconnection can disrupt our body's natural balance, leading to an accumulation of positive ions. These charged molecules may originate from sources such as smartphones, TVs, Wi-Fi routers, air pollution, poor ventilation, and synthetic materials, which may contribute to disruption and dysregulation of the body.

Grounding, or earthing, is the simple act of reconnecting with the Earth by allowing your body to come into direct contact with it. The Earth carries negative ions that help neutralise the positive ions we gather from daily life. This exchange supports your body's natural balance, stabilising your internal environment and helping to regulate your biological clock, circadian rhythms, and cortisol levels.

Grounding offers a range of potential benefits, including:

- reduced inflammation
- lower stress levels
- balanced hormones
- pain relief
- increased energy
- improved sleep quality

ACTION STEP: Incorporate grounding into your everyday routine with these simple activities:

- Walk barefoot on grass, sand, or soil.
- Sit or lie on the ground and feel the Earth beneath you.
- Spend time at the beach.
- Swim in natural bodies of water.
- Garden with your hands in the soil.

33. Forgive Yourself

We all navigate life with the tools, knowledge, and capacity we have at any given moment. Mistakes are part of being human; perfection isn't the goal. Our choices and actions are shaped by the insights and energy available to us at the time. Instead of dwelling on where you feel you fell short, recognise your efforts given the circumstances. Stop beating yourself up for mistakes or perceived shortcomings. Commend yourself for doing the best you could and for your ability to self-reflect. When we know better, we can do better, and that is no small thing!

ACTION STEP:

- Pause and reflect: Pay attention to your self-talk. Are you being overly critical?

- Practice self-compassion: When you notice negative self-talk, challenge it. Be kinder to yourself. You're doing the best you can.

- Celebrate progress: Write down three ways you've shown growth or resilience.

- Create a forgiveness ritual: If you're holding onto guilt or regret, write it down on a piece of paper. Spend a moment reflecting, then forgive yourself. Tear it up or safely burn it as a symbolic act of letting it go.

Be gentle with yourself. Forgiveness is a powerful act of self-love, and you deserve it.

34. Flow

Have you ever become so absorbed in an activity that you lost all track of time? This state of total focus is known as *flow*, a term coined by psychologist Mihaly Csikszentmihalyi. In flow, you're deeply engaged and relaxed, yet focused. When in flow, you might forget about the outside world, and time seems to slip away.

Experiencing flow is linked to increased happiness, creativity, productivity, and a sense of accomplishment. This state can also activate the parasympathetic nervous system, which calms the body, reduces stress, and enhances emotional regulation.

You might experience flow during creative activities like painting, writing, cooking, sewing, playing music, or crafting; physical pursuits such as running, yoga, dancing, or sport; or mindful practices like meditation, gardening, woodworking, or spending time in nature. Tasks that involve problem-solving or require deep focus and skill can also lead to a flow state.

ACTION STEP: Take a moment to reflect upon when you last experienced flow. What activity were you engaged in? Was it creative, physical, or a task requiring your full attention? Now, consider how you can invite more flow into your life: Set aside uninterrupted time to focus on activities that enhance creativity and curiosity. Reduce Distraction by leaving your phone in another room and choosing a quiet environment away from others.

35. Be Kind

Each day, we interact with family, friends, neighbours, colleagues, and strangers, often wearing our "best face" to navigate the demands of life. But beneath the surface, everyone carries unseen challenges, personal struggles, emotional burdens, and pain that we may never fully understand.

In daily life, stress, differing opinions, and misunderstandings are inevitable. It's easy to react in frustration or assume the worst about someone's behaviour. The truth is, so much goes on below the surface of every interaction, things we are not privy to and might never know unless we take the time to ask.

Kindness is one of the simplest yet most profound gifts we can offer. It doesn't mean ignoring boundaries or accepting harmful behaviour, but choosing empathy over judgment. Extending grace and understanding lightens someone else's load and brings us a greater sense of peace.

ACTION STEP: Cut others some slack. When someone's actions seem confusing or hurtful, remind yourself that you don't know their whole story. Take a breath and choose kindness instead of assuming intent. Ask yourself, "How can I respond with compassion instead of frustration?" Whether it's a warm smile to a stranger, a patient response in a heated moment, or simply holding space for someone else's struggles, kindness costs nothing but can transform lives, yours included.

36. Reframe

The brain has evolved to keep us safe by making sense of the world and our relationships. It interprets our experiences through emotions, physical sensations, memories, and beliefs. However, these interpretations may not always be accurate. Our perceptions can be shaped, and sometimes distorted, by past experiences, cultural and societal influences, personal values, and stress levels.

Though the mind creates meaning to protect us, it is important to question its messages. Our inner dialogue can significantly impact how we feel and how we interact with others. Stressful thoughts can fuel judgment, low mood, anxiety, and anger. Over time, persistent negativity triggers stress hormones that disrupt sleep, weaken immunity, and strain relationships.

ACTION STEP: Recognise when you're spiralling into unhelpful thinking. Take a breath, centre yourself and lean into curiosity. Challenge the thought by asking what else could be true here. For example, instead of "I didn't hear back from my friend, they must be upset with me." Try "Perhaps they have a lot going on?" It's okay to ask questions to clarify. Be open to revisiting the meaning you give things and recognise that initial interpretations may not be accurate. By exploring alternative possibilities, you make space for emotional regulation, more effective communication and a stronger connection with others.

37. Eating an Elephant

"How do you eat an elephant? One bite at a time" is a well-known metaphor for breaking down overwhelming tasks into manageable steps. I've had moments where the size of a task felt completely overwhelming. When I set out to create a website and publish this book, I had no idea where to begin. Both felt intimidating enough to make me want to give up altogether.

Instead of letting the size of these undertakings defeat me, I chose a different approach. I committed to working on them for 30 minutes a day. Some days, I barely made any progress. Other days, I got lost in the flow and spent much longer than planned, but by showing up consistently, day after day, I was able to bring these visions to life.

Over time, small, consistent efforts add up. Whether it's working toward a professional goal, improving your finances, or losing weight, each small, intentional step can move you closer to where you aspire to be.

ACTION STEP: Identify something you'd like to achieve or need to get done. What's one small, consistent action you could take towards it? Commit to starting and then do it again the next day. With steady, consistent effort, even the most daunting things become possible.

38. Fuel Your Brain

The brain uses approximately 20% of the energy the body produces, so providing it with proper fuel is essential for maintaining daily focus and energy. Staying well-hydrated is just as important for brain health. Be sure to keep a water bottle handy and sip regularly throughout the day to support mental clarity and physical vitality.

Some brain-boosting food groups to include each day are:

- Protein: Think lean meats, fatty fish, eggs, or a handful of nuts to keep your brain sharp.

- Good Fats: Healthy fats are crucial. Include avocado, extra-virgin olive oil, coconut oil, flaxseeds, pumpkin seeds, or chia seeds for sustained energy.

- Fruits & Veggies: Broccoli, leafy greens, blueberries, and bananas are packed with nutrients that support brain function.

- Smart Snacks: Easy options, such as carrots and hummus, offer a satisfying and nutritious boost between meals.

ACTION STEP: Consider eating a variety of the above to fuel your brain and maintain steady energy throughout the day.

39. Inner Child

Each of us has an inner child. The part of us that is deeply tied to emotion, creativity, and wonder. It reflects our most authentic self, and also holds our unresolved fears, unmet needs, and wounds. As adults, we often neglect this part of ourselves, leaving it feeling unheard or rejected. This can surface as moodiness, frustration, or reactiveness.

By connecting with our inner child, we invite greater emotional freedom, joy, and authenticity. This curious, playful part of us holds the key to deeper fulfilment. Honouring it fosters self-compassion and opens the door to healing.

Signs your inner child needs attention:

- You feel overly sensitive or reactive to criticism. Often, our strongest emotional responses are echoes from the past.
- You struggle to set boundaries or feel guilty for prioritising yourself.
- You have difficulty expressing emotions or asking for what you need.
  You feel disconnected from joy, creativity, or spontaneity.

ACTION STEP: Reconnect with your inner child:

1. Set aside quiet time: To tune in to your inner child. This could be through journaling, meditating, or simply sitting in a peaceful space.

2. Ask open-ended questions: Gently ask yourself questions like:
   - What is my inner child trying to tell me?
   - What unmet needs are coming up?
   - How can I offer comfort, reassurance, or joy to this part of myself?

3. Engage in play: Recall activities you enjoyed as a child and make time for them. Whether it's painting, dancing, building, or exploring.

4. Practice self-compassion: Treat yourself with kindness and patience. Validate your feelings. Remind yourself that it's okay to take care of yourself.

5. Create rituals: Establish regular practices that nurture the child within. Read a favourite childhood book or watch a nostalgic movie

6. Write a letter to your inner child: Use your dominant hand to write as your adult self. Allow your inner child to respond using your non-dominant hand.

7. Re-parent your inner child: Offer yourself in the present moment, the words of reassurance, understanding, soothing, and comfort that your younger self may have needed to receive long ago but did not.

8. Seek professional support: If your inner child is carrying significant pain or trauma, consider working with a therapist to help navigate this in a safe and supportive environment.

40. Banish the Word Busy

Jacqui Lewis talks about 'banishing busy' in her book, *14-Day Mind Cleanse*. Busy has become a way of life for many. With the constant pressure to always be 'doing' and squeeze more and more into our days. We find ourselves juggling multiple responsibilities and multitasking in all areas of our life; however, this constant busyness isn't always beneficial.

Continually using the word 'busy' tends to become an unhelpful, self-fulfilling prophecy. It's often the first word we respond with when someone asks how we are. Whilst it may be true, it perpetuates the idea that constant doing is normal, even if it's not working for us. We may begin to measure our worth by how much we're doing, rather than on the quality or meaning of the tasks. Reframing how we speak about our time helps us reclaim a greater sense of agency over how we live and work.

ACTION STEP: Replace the word "busy" with "productive." Being productive means you are actually getting things done. Set clear, realistic goals for the day. Start with your top priorities and let go of the idea that everything must be done today. Acknowledge what you accomplish, no matter how small, and focus on one thing at a time. When you shift your perspective from "busy" to "productive," you enhance your effectiveness and create more space for calm.

41. Reflect

Take quiet moments to reflect, whether it's after a conversation, after navigating a tricky moment, or as you wind down at the end of the day. Check in with yourself. What stood out? What felt good? What would you do differently next time?

ACTION STEP: Consider:

- What went well?
- What didn't go as planned?
- What made you feel proud?
- Where would you like to improve or grow?
- What new insights could help as you move forward?
- Do you need to ask for help?

Be honest and compassionate with yourself. It's not about being hard on yourself. It's about noticing, learning from experience, and choosing who you want to be moving forward.

42. Be Present

Have you ever noticed how your body can be in one place, while your mind is elsewhere? Whether we're rehashing the past or worrying about the future, this constant mental drifting can lead to feeling scattered and disconnected from the moment.

When you're fully present, you're more engaged with your experiences, relationships, and surroundings, which can lead to greater happiness and a more profound sense of calm.

Being present is about gently anchoring yourself in the here and now and paying attention to where you are, what you're doing, and who you're with.

ACTION STEP: When you catch yourself lost in thought or feeling all over the place, try these techniques to bring your focus back to the present moment:

Engage your senses:

- Notice the taste of your food or drink.
- Feel the texture of your clothing or the warmth of the sun.
- Listen to the sounds around you, like birdsong, or the hum of life.
- Look for the different colours you can see in your surroundings.

Reconnect with your body:

- Pay attention to your breath - feel the rise and fall of your chest.
- Move mindfully - whether it's walking, stretching, or even washing the dishes, notice how your body feels as you move.

Be present with others:

- Focus on the people you're with. Look them in the eye, listen deeply to what they're saying, ask questions, and engage fully in the conversation.

The more you practise being present, the easier it becomes to quieten the mental chatter and fully experience life as it unfolds. Over time, you'll likely find yourself feeling more grounded, regulated, and in tune with the world around you.

43. Replenish

Just as a car needs fuel to keep running, we too need to refuel ourselves to stay balanced, motivated, and capable of meeting life's demands. Recognising when you're feeling depleted is the first step. Make space for the things that uplift and replenish you. That could be connecting with loved ones, spending time outside, enjoying a creative pursuit, or taking time for yourself.

ACTION STEP: What restores and replenishes your energy? Ask yourself:

- Which activities leave me feeling refreshed and recharged?
- Who in my life uplifts and supports me?
- Which environments help me feel relaxed and grounded?

Once you've identified these sources of replenishment, commit to prioritising them. Schedule time to connect with someone you care about, plan a visit to a favourite place, or disconnect from the world for a while. Treat these moments as essential, because they are.

44. Do What Lights You Up

Doing what lights you up is about connecting with and following those things, big or small, that make you smile, or create a spark of inner happiness, joy or wonder. They are the people, places, and experiences that you feel drawn towards. These seemingly small moments are often clues pointing to the callings of your soul. When you follow them, you begin to create a life of alignment.

Rebecca Campbell discusses this concept in her book *Light Is the New Black*, where she shares how she began regularly buying peonies, her favourite flower, as a joyous weekly ritual. This small act became a way of reconnecting with herself and honouring what made her happy. She goes on to describe how she also spent time sitting in her local park journaling her thoughts, realisations, and inspirations and then sharing those reflections on social media. This practice eventually led to her writing books, speaking, and stepping onto a whole new, soul-led career path.

ACTION STEP: Notice what sparks curiosity and happiness within you. What are you drawn towards or curious to explore? Your happiness matters. Trust your inner guidance system and let it lead you to experiences that feel authentic and reflect who you truly are.

45. Seek Support

Our family, friends, and colleagues can be wonderful sources of comfort and encouragement during tough times. However, there are moments when the support we need goes beyond what our loved ones can realistically provide. Professional support can provide a safe, skilled space to work through ongoing or more complex challenges.

Likewise, bottling things up, pretending everything is fine and trying to navigate tough times entirely on your own can take a significant toll. It's okay not to have all the answers and to need help. Reaching out doesn't mean you're failing; it means you're human.

If you're finding it difficult to cope or if certain emotions or thoughts feel persistent, consider reaching out for additional help. Seeking support is a courageous and responsible step that allows you to care for yourself while maintaining healthy, balanced relationships with others. If the first practitioner you see is not a good fit, keep looking until you find someone who is. I saw twelve doctors before I found someone who could truly help. Keep going until you find a healthcare professional who feels right for you. It's worth it.

ACTION STEP: If you're experiencing grief, loss, change, chronic stress, anxiety, depression, illness, or simply feeling overwhelmed and struggling to cope, consider reaching out to your GP or a counsellor. You're not alone, and help is available. If cost is a concern, look for free support services in your area. Lifeline and Beyond Blue are available in Australia.

46. Explore Somewhere New

Exploring somewhere new is an excellent way to blow out the cobwebs and refresh your mind, body, and spirit. It allows us to break free from routine, create memories, and have fun. Whether it's somewhere local, a nearby town or a distant city, this act of discovery awakens a sense of curiosity and the adventurer within. It invites us to embrace the unfamiliar and step outside of our comfort zone, enabling us to cultivate a deeper connection to the world around us and to nourish our souls.

ACTION STEP: Choose a new destination and aim to experience it fully. Consider using a different mode of transport than usual to add to the adventure. See if you can tick off these three things while you're there:

1. **BUY something:** Whether it's a local craft or a small memento.

2. **DO something:** Visit a museum, take a walk, or try a new activity.

3. **EAT something:** Try a dish you haven't had before from a local eatery.

47. Tune In

Your body constantly communicates with you, offering subtle (and sometimes not-so-subtle) messages about what it needs. Learning to tune in and truly listen can transform your physical and emotional wellbeing.

The idea of "embodiment" has gained momentum as a way to calm the nervous system and return to the present moment. At its core, embodiment simply means being present *to* and *within* your body. Given the way most of us live our lives, it's easy to miss the signals of stress, pleasure, hunger, or exhaustion. We override these cues, pushing through tiredness, ignoring thirst, or turning to food or drink for comfort, without realising what the body is trying to tell us. In truth, our body holds every thought, emotion, and experience we've ever had.

Taking time to tune in helps us recognise what we need before illness or burnout takes hold. Try letting your body lead the way before your mind jumps in to override it or figure things out. The more present you become, the safer and more at home you'll feel in your own skin. When you create space to listen, your body will guide you toward better balance and greater trust in yourself.

At the beginning of my journey toward body awareness, I read *The Body Love Diet* by Ingrid Arna. At the start of the book, there's a short but powerful affirmation that serves as a simple reminder that healing often begins with listening, appreciation and love. It reads:

"Body, you are amazing! I send you my deep appreciation. I am going to love you, and love you, and love you. I trust you and thank you for taking such good care of me."

ACTION STEP:

1. Settle yourself: Find a quiet, comfortable spot where you won't be disturbed. Sit or lie down in a relaxed position.

2. Connect with your heart: Place your hands on your heart, take slow, deep breaths in and out, and allow your body to relax.

3. Ask and listen: Gently ask yourself, "Body, what do you need right now?" Stay open to whatever sensations, emotions, or thoughts arise.

4. Respond with care: Honour what your body asks for, whether it's rest, nourishment, movement, or connection.

5. Make it a habit: Revisit this practice regularly to strengthen your connection with yourself and cultivate a more profound sense of awareness. The more you tune in, the more attuned you'll become to your own body's wisdom.

48. Focus on What You Can Control

By focusing on what you can influence, you empower yourself to navigate life's challenges more gracefully. It is easy at times to get swept up in the chaos and feel like we're at the mercy of what is happening around us. But when we stop trying to influence or manage what isn't ours to carry, and focus instead on our own thoughts, behaviour and choices. We begin to feel more in charge of our own experience.

My father often reminded me of the simple wisdom of *The Serenity Prayer*. Taking a moment to reflect on these words has helped me find calm and refocus.

"God, grant me the serenity.
To accept the things I cannot change.
The courage to change the things I can,
and the wisdom to know the difference."

ACTION STEP: Take a moment to consider what is within your control. Note one or two small, actionable steps to address these areas. Then, consciously release the things outside your influence. When you feel overwhelmed, revisit *The Serenity Prayer* (or a similar mantra that resonates with you) to help you recalibrate and regain perspective.

49. Music

Music has the power to lift our spirits and shape our emotional state. Whether it's the rhythm, lyrics, or melody, music can inspire, calm, and energise us in ways that words alone cannot. During difficult times, the right song can serve as a powerful reminder of our inner strength and resilience.

When I was at my sickest, fighting to regain my health, I discovered a song that became my anthem, '*Warrior*' by Havana Brown. It became a symbol of determination. Every time I listened to it, I was reminded of the strength, resolve, and ability we humans have to overcome adversity. It was a lifeline that helped me focus on my recovery goal and my ability to achieve it.

Music can serve as a motivational tool, especially when you need to boost your mood or tap into your inner resilience. Music can remind you of who you are and what you're capable of, whether it's a track that makes you feel empowered or one that fills you with joy.

ACTION STEP: Identify a song (or several!) that carries the message or energy you need right now. It could be a song that boosts your confidence, reminds you of your strength, or simply uplifts you. Make it your go-to soundtrack for difficult moments or create a playlist of empowering songs that inspire you. Play it often. Let the music work its magic to change your mood and mindset.

50. Sleep Sanctuary

The ancient Egyptians regarded sleep as a sacred state, deeply connected to spiritual and physical wellbeing. They believed sleep was a gateway to the divine, a time when prophetic dreams could bring guidance and rejuvenate the body and soul.

Sleep allows the body and mind to recharge. It helps the brain to function correctly, improving concentration, clear thinking, and memory. It promotes cardiac health and regulates blood sugar. A good night's sleep boosts the immune system, reduces inflammation, regulates hormones, and supports emotional health.

ACTION STEP: Treat your sleep as sacred, like the Egyptians did. Establish an evening routine that allows your body to wind down and prepare adequately for sleep. Shawn Stevenson, in his book *Sleep Smarter,* suggests the following:

Prepare your body for sleep:

- Switch off screens and devices at least an hour before bedtime.
- Get to bed at the right time. Staying up late with lights on is not natural for the body. Melatonin naturally starts to rise when the sun sets. Aim to be in bed between 9 pm and 11 pm to catch the body's natural rise.
- Have a warm bath or shower before bed to relax and prepare for sleep.

- Calm the mind. Journal, read a book, focus on your breath, meditate.
- Get some sunlight during the day.
- Set a caffeine, sugar, and additive curfew each day, nothing after 2 pm.
- Mentally recap the day. Note what you are grateful for and proud of yourself for.

Prepare your bedroom for sleep:

- Dim the lights, draw the blinds, close the door, and wear an eye mask. Light sources of any kind can disrupt sleep; do what you need to minimise them.
- Get the room temperature just right. We sleep better in a slightly cooler environment; approximately 20°C (68°F) is recommended.
- Put a couple of drops of good-quality lavender essential oil on your pillow.
- Keep laptops, phones and other devices out of the bedroom.
- Indoor plants can improve air quality; consider having some in the bedroom.

51. Treat Yourself

You deserve good things, not someday, but every day! When you prioritise your happiness, even in small ways, you're nurturing your spirit, recharging your battery and reconnecting with what brings you fulfilment.

All too often, we put our own needs on the back burner. But what if you didn't have to wait for the weekend, a special occasion, or a well-deserved holiday to indulge in the little things that fill you up?

Do things just for you, things that feel like a treat or an indulgence, which are fun or nourishing in some way. It could be taking the scenic route, buying yourself a fancy coffee, laughing out loud at a comedy show, or savouring a quiet moment with a good book. Whatever feels like a treat, however small, is your invitation to show yourself that you matter.

ACTION STEP: Pick one small thing that feels indulgent and joyful. Maybe it's buying concert tickets, taking a warm bath, or indulging in your favourite treat. Whatever it is, let it remind you that you're worth the time, energy, and love it takes to care for yourself every single day.

52. Prayer Jar

Letting go of what weighs us down isn't always easy. Sometimes it is the simplest practices that bring unexpected comfort. Some years ago, I began writing down my worries on small pieces of paper, offering them up as silent prayers. Each note was placed into a glass jar, a symbolic gesture of handing them over to the Divine, trusting that what I could not control would be lovingly held and tended to.

Every few months, I take time to revisit those prayers. I give thanks for the ones that have been answered and gently return those still in progress to the jar. This small ritual has helped me release anxiety and cultivate trust in both the unseen and in the natural unfolding of life.

ACTION STEP: Find an empty jar, box, or any container that feels special to you. Set aside a quiet moment to write down what's weighing upon your heart, one worry or prayer per piece of paper. Add the date. As you place each note into the jar, take a breath and release it, offering it up with gratitude and trust.

Return to your jar now and then, not just to check on your prayers but to acknowledge progress, express gratitude, and remind yourself that you are not alone in the challenges you face.

Notes

Notes

Notes

*"A good laugh and a long sleep
are two of the best cures for anything"*

-Irish Proverb

Final Thoughts

I hope this little book has inspired you to reflect, reset, and reimagine how you might better prioritise and care for yourself, and that it helps you to place your wellbeing at the centre of your life, rather than treating it as an afterthought. You are someone who is truly worthy of your own time, attention, and devotion.

While many of the ideas shared here are simple, I recognise that integrating them into daily life isn't always easy. Real change requires patience, consistency, and self-kindness. Prioritising your wellbeing might stretch you in new ways. It may require you to let go of old habits, slow down, or rethink your current routines. At times, that might feel daunting. So I encourage you to begin gently. Start small, take it one step at a time. There's no need to do everything all at once. Choose just one thing and do it intentionally and consistently. That's how sustainable change happens. Every day, in every moment, you have the chance to begin again. To make a different choice that's more aligned with who you are, what you need, and the kind of life you wish to create.

The journey of personal wellbeing is something that unfolds across a lifetime, offering us the freedom to experiment, adjust, and realign with what nourishes us throughout our lives. As I mentioned at the beginning of this book, the strategies and practices I've shared here were developed over a decade. To this day, they are a work in progress and continue to evolve in response to my own needs and changing life circumstances.

You, too, get to shape a path that honours your needs, your body, and your circumstances. One that is flexible enough to meet you where you are. Life doesn't always go the way we imagine it will. Plans change, doors close, and new chapters begin unexpectedly. But even when the path looks different from what we envisioned, it can still be rich with meaning, connection, and fulfilment. The unexpected version of life can have a depth and beauty that we might never have found on the path we'd planned.

What matters most is that you continue to show up for yourself with curiosity and kindness. It is my heartfelt wish that you will move forward with deeper self-awareness and the courage and commitment to live in a way that truly supports you.

Acknowledgements

A huge and special thank you to my beta readers - John Bray, Di Dalziel, Jackie Dalziel, Cathy Polities, and Jo Stower - for so generously offering your time, thoughtful insights, and invaluable feedback. Your suggestions helped to elevate this work, and I am deeply grateful for your time, encouragement and support. Thank you so very much.

To my husband, Joe - thank you for believing in me, your honesty that keeps me grounded, and for your love, loyalty, encouragement and support through every chapter of our lives together. What an unexpected ride it's been!

About The Author

Emma has been a dedicated teacher since 2001, with a diverse career spanning both rural and metropolitan schools across South East Queensland, Australia. During her career, Emma has faced burnout and overcome seemingly insurmountable health challenges, which have given her a deeper understanding of how wellbeing is shaped by more than just physical health. She now brings this insight into her own life and encourages others as they navigate their wellbeing paths.

Emma holds a Bachelor of Education and additional qualifications in Wellness Coaching, and blends her teaching expertise with a deep commitment to health and wellness. She supports and facilitates personal and workplace wellbeing initiatives with a particular focus on teacher wellbeing.

When not in the classroom, Emma enjoys spending time with her husband and beloved dogs. She loves reading, cooking, travelling, the quiet comfort of home, and rich connection with others. She continues to actively integrate wellbeing practices into all aspects of her daily life.

Find Emma on Instagram @nurture_for_you

References

Arna, Ingrid (2010) *The Body Love Diet ebook* - https://bodylovedietbook.com/

Campbell, R. (2015). *Light is the new black: A guide to answering your soul's callings and working your light.* Hay House.

Carlaw, Lise & Wills, Sarah (2022) *Forty Favours the Brave,* Finch Publishing, Australia

Cody, Nicole (2024) *Journey Maker Planner.* Journey Maker Press (Starship 7 Pty Ltd).

Dalton-Smith, Saundra (2017*) Sacred Rest: Recover Your Life, Renew Your Energy, Restore Your Sanity*, Faithwords, Hatchette Book Group

Green, Amy (2022) *'Teacher Wellbeing – A Real Conversation for Teachers and Leaders'* Amba Press, Melbourne, Australia

Lewis, Jacqui (2022) *'The 14 Day Mind Cleanse'*, Murdoch Books, Sydney, Australia

Csikszentmihalyi, Mihaly. (1990). *Flow: The psychology of optimal experience.* Harper & Row.

My Wellbeing Teacher Planner (2024) Teachers 4 Teachers, Taren Point, Australia

Neff, Kristin (2011). *Self-compassion: The proven power of being kind to yourself.* William Morrow.

Popovic, Helena (2024) 'The Joys of Looking Forward', Life Matters Podcast episode, 5 Nov, ABC Listen

Scher, A. B. (2016). *How to heal yourself when no one else can: A total self-healing approach for mind, body, and spirit.* Llewellyn Worldwide

Shawn Stevenson (2016) *Sleep Smarter – 21 Essential Strategies to sleep your way to a better body, better health, and bigger success*' Hay House Australia, Alexandria, Australia

Williams, Mark. A. (2023). *The connected species: How the evolution of the human brain can save the world.* Rowman & Littlefield Publishers.

https://www.emed.com.au/nutrition/optimal-water-intake/

https://www.psychologytoday.com/us/blog/click-here-for-happiness/201901/what-is-well-being-definition-types-and-well-being-skills

https://lovinglifeco.com/health-and-wellbeing/the-role-of-hydration-in-maintaining-overall-health-and-wellbeing/

https://www.who.int/

Printed in Dunstable, United Kingdom